Extraordinary in The Ordinary

Extraordinary in The Ordinary

J. Pittman McGehee

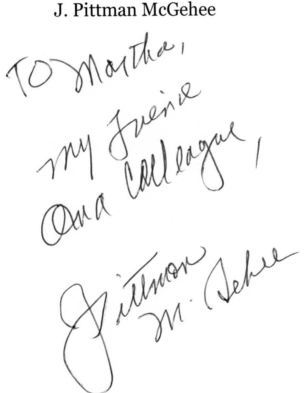

To Martha,
my friend
and colleague,

Pittman
M. Gehee

LITERARY PRESS
LAMAR UNIVERSITY

ISBN: 978-1-942956-39-6
Library of Congress Control Number: 2017930853

Cover Art: Merrilee McGehee
Book Design: Erin Lanier

Lamar University Literary Press
Beaumont, Texas

Acknowledgments

First and foremost to Jerry Craven, Press Director, at Lamar University Literary Press, for putting my poetry in publication. And further for what he has done for Texas Poetry in general. I would like to thank Jazz Jaeschke who transcribed this work from handwritten to typed poems. For her tireless reading and typing I offer much thanks. Further, to Erin Lanier for her clean and clear editing. Finally to my very creative daughter-in-law, Merrilee McGehee for her beautiful cover design. Without the above, this book would never have happened.

Poetry from Lamar University Literary Press

Bobby Aldridge, *An Affair of the Stilled Heart*
Michael Baldwin, *Lone Star Heart, Poems of a Life in Texas*
Charles Behlen, *Failing Heaven*
Alan Berecka, *With Our Baggage*
David Bowles, *Flower, Song, Dance: Aztec and Mayan Poetry*
Jerry Bradley, *Crownfeathers and Effigies*
Jerry Bradley and Ulf Kirchdorfer, editors, *The Great American Wise Ass Poetry Anthology*
Matthew Brennan, *One Life*
Paul Christensen, *The Jack of Diamonds is a Hard Card to Play*
Christopher Carmona, Rob Johnson, and Chuck Taylor, editors, *The Beatest State in the Union*
Chip Dameron, *Waiting for an Etcher*
William Virgil Davis, *The Bones Poems*
Jeffrey DeLotto, *Voices Writ in Sand*
Chris Ellery, *Elder Tree*
Mimi Ferebee, *Wildfires and Atmospheric Memories*
Larry Griffin, *Cedar Plums*
Ken Hada, *Margaritas and Redfish*
Michelle Hartman, *Disenchanted and Disgruntled*
Michelle Hartman, *Irony and Irreverence*
Katherine Hoerth, *Goddess Wears Cowboy Boots*
Lynn Hoggard, *Motherland*
Gretchen Johnson, *A Trip Through Downer, Minnesota*
Ulf Kirchdorfer, *Chewing Green Leaves*
Laozi, *Daodejing*, tr. By David Breeden, Steven Schroeder, and Wally Swist
Janet McCann, *The Crone at the Casino*
Erin Murphy, *Ancilla*
Laurence Musgrove, *Local Bird*
Dave Oliphant, *The Pilgrimage, Selected Poems: 1962-2012*
Kornelijus Platelis, *Solitary Architectures*
Carol Coffee Reposa, *Underground Musicians*
Jan Seale, *The Parkinson Poems*
Steven Schroeder, *the moon, not the finger, pointing*
Carol Smallwood, *Water, Earth, Air, Fire, and Picket Fences*
Glen Sorestad *Hazards of Eden*
W.K. Stratton, *Ranchero Ford/ Dying in Red Dirt Country*
Wally Swist, *Invocation*
Jonas Zdanys (ed.), *Pushing the Envelope, Epistolary Poems*
Jonas Zdanys, *Red Stones*

For information on these and other Lamar University Literary Press books go to
www.Lamar.edu/literarypress

For

My Wife, Bobby

Sons, Pittman and Jarrett

Daughters-in-law, Merrilee and Leigh Ann

Grandchildren, Finnegan, Baxter, Clementine, and Quinton

A poem has secrets that the poet knows nothing of.
—Stanley Kunitz

CONTENTS

Matter

There are two world views that
matter: everything matters;
nothing matters. Each enfolds
into the other. So it is, that in the
first, every heart beat and breath
drawn matters. Living mindfully
in the moment means that each second
is second to none. Taste, touch, sound,
smell and sight are Blake's inlets
into the Soul. Every moment is
a movement into the whole, where
everything matters. Don't miss
a single second, not an eye blink
of beauty even in the mundane or
ordinary. So this view reigns.
The twin view accepts that we are a
third rate Planet, in a second rate
Universe. The cosmos beyond
comprehension , therefore our lives are
a blip on a universal screen. All
those things that produce fear,
anxiety and dread, are of
no consequence in the grand scope.
Let it go. A century from now
what will matter about your
tentative and temporary life?
Feeling devalued? The value
is in the relief that nothing
matters ... not even matter,
for it too will cease. So
my life matters. And not at all.
Can two things be true at
once, which are opposites?
Hold the two. When anxiety
and dread dominate, go to the
second view. When the second

view leaves you sad and lonely
crawl toward the first.
When the first makes you
anxious and dreadful, run
toward the second. Or hold the
two until they are one.

Lent 1/16 ✦
Words Over Wounds

So I commit to a
poem a day. Discipline,
play, purpose server,
anti-depressant? Ritual

process, superstition,
or it is the pouring of
words over wounds, healing
sounds, like the brief wind

from an angel's wing or
the breath of a four-year-
old's laugh. More so the

breeze at five A.M. off
the balcony rail when
day dawns again.

Beware — Be Aware

Ithaca was never the
goal, but the occasion
for the journey. Tolkien
penned "Not all who wander
are lost." So much for
the presumption that what
we seek will be found. It
will not. But, if we seek
such, it will find us.

Beware of poems that
preach. Be aware of poems
that point to truth, even
when fiction is the true
form to find the pearl.
Go to Ithaca, wander
where life's labyrinth
leads, knowing that if
you keep moving you

will reach the center.

Words

Words are symbols chasing
concepts they will never catch.
Because we name something
doesn't mean we know it.
One of life's great paradoxes
is that things about which
we cannot speak, we must!

The unspeakable. Is to
speak. Can we not conclude
that the most meaningful
human values are difficult
to express? God, Soul,
love, let's start there. Meister
Eckhart says, "The only image

of God, is no image." If
we cannot conceive of God
why would we seek a Con-
cept? So we seek synonyms.
Transcendent, Sacred, Holy, Mystery,
Meaning, Numinous, Presence.
None of which capture the whole

And what of Soul? The
essence that is seated at
center and circumference.
Essence and totality, personal
and transpersonal. We know
Soul and can never define it.
This is the truth of this poem.

The truth is that words do
not comprehend. I will
not speak of love. How
could that one word

possibly address the
world's greatest mystery.
So there is a word that

attempts to describe
God, Soul, love. Mystery
must be the mother of meaning.
Out of her comes that which
we seek. It is our birth
and death, two words meaning
extremes that are one ... words!

Eliminate The Light

If it were made law that a
poem could not contain
the word or image of
light, then the poet's pens

would run dry. So what
must we learn from such
a fantasy?   Maybe the
poet of this poem is a

light-weight. Wasn't the
premise a ponderable
proposition. Light is
a symbol of sight and

insight. Light can ignite.
Solar energy manifests
before lunar light and
they are the same. The light

is a synonym for revelation.
It is a resource of the
Source. When the poet
writes of the light one
imagines the crack in
the drape cutting across
the room. Without light

we would never have had
a starry starry night.
Painting and poem portray
pillars of light. So now,

we know, light is Source and
resource for the poet and
the life trying to be portrayed.

Perhaps for another poem we
could speculate how
if light were illegal in a poem
how we could never know of

the Dark.

Large Discovery

I have spent some time
trying to write a small
poem, only to discover
that there is no such thing.
There may be short poems,
but no poem is small.

Rose Window

Why do we humans build
grand cathedrals and then
bomb them? We humans
do embody creativity and

destructiveness. Those more
profound than I have opined
about life's paired opposites
and how both must be present

for evolution. I love the
Glazier who put the stained
glass shard high on the rose
window knowing no human

would ever see it. That
can't be destroyed, it
is fully evolved. God
saw it!

Take It Easy
In Memory of Glen Frey

"Standing on the corner in Winslow
Arizona, and such a fine sight to see,
It's a girl, my Lord, in a flatbed Ford
Slowin' down to take a look at me."

It is hard not to love a song that
Sings of Soul in a truck, as the Incarnation:
"It's a girl, my Lord ..."
Philip told Nathaniel that the Messiah

Had come and was in Nazareth. "Can
Anything good come from Nazareth?"
Philip said, "Come and see."
Lord, girl, flatbed Ford ... Why not!?

Have the Incarnation appear on the
Corner in Winslow Arizona? The truth
Flies through like an Eagle. Your love
Will save me. The choice is easy: Climb in.

With a world of trouble on my mind,
The Lord loosened my load and I am gonna,
Take it easy!

Leisurely Lunch

So, what is better than a
leisurely lunch. First the
cold, frosty glass of Chardonnay.
Then, crack the book of poetry

brought to stimulate. Milosz,
Neruda, Nye, Eliot and Oliver:
hors d'oeuvres. Then the
bruschetta. Olive oil, garlic,
tomatoes, herbs set the stage for
a rehearsal of the spiritual

practice of a leisurely lunch.
So, now, the second glass
of sacramental wine. Buttery
the Chardonnay, not as in butter,
but as in smooth, like when
your tongue licks your lips to
find the second taste. There

is no entrée, for the entire
is entry into a singular ex-
perience of the whole. Wine,
bead, familiar elements.
All revealed in a café near
you where the leisurely lunch is
dependent on you and your attitude.

A Rope Called Hope

I listened to a woman today
who has had the worst human
experience: her child died by suicide.
Fingers entwined, she wrung her hands

as the story unfolded. It was
as if the glow of soul was on a
rheostat, and the light behind
her eyes grew dim. Staying present

to the account and sending empathic
energy to her, I found my
fingers locked in a boney weave.
We held the space for the grief

to find its grip in our hands
held in a healing grasp for
something to hang onto, like

a rope called hope.

Taste

My son and I decided to
split an order of twelve.

Oysters are not an acquired
taste, they are a required taste.

Not so much for the taste,
though for us, sublime,

but for the image of the
look on the face of the person

who ate the first oyster.
This shelled, slimy, oily

organism can be a
vehicle for the Transcendent

to become immanent.
You know, Divine.

It is, after all, a matter
of taste.

Non-Sentimental Journey

Home is an archetype, that
is to say, the same longing
for each of us. Such irony.
A place we must make and
a place we must leave and
a place to which we
long to return. Joseph
Campbell wrote of the
Hero's Journey: Separation,
initiation, return. We
must leave home, be trans-
formed by the journey and
return home. Elliott says,
"After all our exploring, we will
return (home) and know it
for the first time." John
Denver sings, "going home to
a place we have never been
before." In baseball, our
National pastime, we leave
home, seeking to return with-
out dying on base. In order
to get home, someone must
sacrifice for us. So there
it is. We all must leave
home. And return again.
Circle, cycle, labyrinth? It
is a non-sentimental journey
and our beginning and our end.

Sacred Solitude

There is a difference between
isolation and solitude. One
neurotic, the other sacred.
They look alike. And this is an

example that attitude is a
state of being, not action.
Solitude is sacred time with
the mind: mindful. Today

I luxuriate in my soli-
tude. I am not by myself,
I am with myself. The
only relationship I

know I will go to the
grave with, is with
me. So, I/we en-
joy. In joy, I see

solitude as sacred.

Behind Quiet Eyes

Where do we go when we sleep?
I do not seek a neurological ex-

planation. I seek to know the
realm of dreams. Where do they

come from. I do not seek a
scientific explanation, I

seek a reflection that
dreams the dream. Dream

maker, dream maker, make
me a dream that unveils

and reveals that there is
a realm beyond time

and space. I know, you

see, because I go there every
night behind quiet eyes.

Wounded God

Tradition names him, "Doubting
Thomas." Not so. I make his
moniker, "Curious Thomas."
His desire to see and touch the
wounds mean to me that he
wanted to know:
      Do we worship a wounded God?

To touch a wounded God is to know
that our wounds are healed.
Scars are signs of healing.
Grace enters the soul through our
wounds. God, too, is wounded.
Disgrace best understands grace.
      Do we worship a wounded God?

Life is loss. We share a scar
at our navel. Such a sign
of death and birth, maternal
twins. Thomas speaks for us all
he was not in doubt, he trusted
his family, but ne needed to know
      Do we worship a wounded God?

Wonderful

At times, when in a
crowd, I wonder what
we are here for. So diff-
erent. So alike. And no
sense of where we come from
or where we are going. Are
we passing time, a human
pastime? Are we contrib-
uting to a mysterious whole
beyond our comprehension?

Occasionally when in a
crowded space, I wonder if
I am the only one wondering.
There seems to be a difference
between wondering and a
sense of wonder. Maybe
one leads to the other. When
that happens, it is wonderful.

wRite

Rite, write, right? This is
much more than the co-
incidence of homonym
in a harmony of words. These
three are for the subtle

conclusion that writing is
a rite, right? My daughter-
in-law taught me this in
a piece of art made of

pencils that spell out,
"wRite". Writing is a ritual,
a rite, the opposite of

wrong. In this context the
opposite of left— might be

the right direction

Illumination

Not everything in the past was
better, though ego's memory
so desires. But, the stars
were. Night prone. That
is, lying on quilts staring
at stars. Constellations,
Milky Way, just the wonder
of such a canopy of light.

So now, occasionally,
when at our summer
cottage or in the
fishing port, I see the
stars. I know why we
use them as metaphors
for one who shines. But,
those who are "stars" are
not. And the true stars
reflect the Solar Source.
That is what truly inspires,
illumination.

Blind Eye

I went for a night walk,
awake or not, made no
difference. I saw that
between the lines there are no
lines. I saw that for which
we sought, sought us.
I saw, though not from
eye sight, but from in-
sight, that the differences
made no difference. I
saw with the soul's
sight that pain informed
us that the system needed
a systematic change.
Sleep walking, awakened
me to be aware that
that which is a dream
may be true, as contrasted
to the small world of
the waking life. Some
insight, from the blind eye.

We Must Remain Silent

Since we cannot conceive of
God, why would we seek a
concept. After all, any refer-
ence to God is our imagi-
nation creating an image.

The image is not God
and speaks more of us
than of God. If horses
have a God, it looks like

a horse. So we seek synon-
yms to point to that about
which we cannot speak.
Holy, Sacred, Divine, Mystery,
Meaning, Other, Numinous,
Presence, Ground of Being,
are all attempts to ex-
press the inexpressible.

So, what shall we say to
these things. Wittgenstein
says: "About those things
which we cannot speak

we must remain silent."
Let us make covenant that
we will only express that
which we experience and

agree that we can name
it whatever we desire:
Holy, Sacred, Divine,
Mystery, Meaning, Other,
Numinous, Presence, Ground
of Being. No name will

name. So feel free,
by any other name,
to not name. "About those things
we cannot speak, we
[may] remain silent.

Meaning

From the birth we did not
request, to the grave we
cannot escape, what
are we to do in the mean-
time, the in-between time?

Mean time. Many meanings
for mean. So we have said,
in between. We have implied
negative action towards
another: "He was mean to me."

"What did she mean by
that?" Mean can mean
a form of praise: "He plays
a mean trumpet." Some-
times it is numerical average.

As I am sure you have
guessed, what we are to
do in the meantime is to
find meaning.

Palliation

Still looking for the
little poem that is
not small, I write:
If you want to palliate
a pain, put it in a poem.

At Intermission

The actresses have fat faces
like mums painted purple and pink.
They overact like they eat.

I watch and wonder, as reality
escapes like street sounds behind
a closing door, why

it bothers me that they sound like
grackles and look like clowns whose
heads are on springs. Staged

reality may be preferable to
real life and popular among
pink and purple mums and

those who watch and wonder at
matinee intermissions at the Plymouth
Theater.

Lazarus

My Lazarus. The rejected me, shoved below
    longing for acceptance. Not satisfied with
    table scraps.

Overwhelming strength within you, you helpless
    adversary judging me in silent vigil out
    side conscious gate.

My ignorance destroys you, killing me, and
    banquet table turns.

Roles reversed, I below, you above and
    I deny why. Blame the sores
    licked by dogs, sickening sores.

Abraham, relieve the agony of my ignorance.
    Do not ignore the beggar, Lazarus.
    Allow him to aid a poor rich man.

No choice left. Gulf is mine, built
    by me. Rejected beggar had his day and
    banquet table takes another turn.

Who will bridge my gap and lick my sores,
    scornful, scary, sickening? Gulf
    eternal. No bridge but to cross.

King

Slim boy searches for himself in a sporting goods store.
Stares at bright baseball caps— alphabet letters on
crowns. A blue one, ears bending under its size and
mother shrieks,

"Put that down now!" Eyes close tightly. Face
squeezes like a prune in pain, puts the cap
back, recoils into the car and tunes in
the radio.

The sky is blue and the air smells fresh like sheets
drying on a clothes line. A wind surfer floats by,
rainbow sail well in hand. Swans— pen, cygnet,
and cob

Swim like paddle boats driven by mysterious
children, invisible and smiling while Beach Boys
sing in a a port town with shops that sell
smoked fish.

My son and his twelve pound salmon—
was a king— on Lake Michigan. That day he
wore a cap and his mother put it on his head
like a crown.

Water Fall

Searching.
New sounds for rocks skipping
across the water he fell
like a frog through the green
thick moss down under the
water where black is dark
blue and his eyes become
pools of truth wet with
visions
making the underworld
water reflective of sounds
shallow surface sounds
echoes
lost in the dark
dark blue
color of his eyes
seeing
where there are no
sounds
of rocks skipping across
the water too deep to be
heard.

Young Urban Professional

A line. Dreamed and
drawn straight from deep
down to shallow
surface. Intersecting
inside.

At Brooks Brothers.
The ties are untied, hanging throatless.
The shirts are held, arms pinned
behind their backs, suffocating in
plastic bags.
The shoes are boxed breathless and
stacked, soles up.
The belts are unbuckled embarrassed
by their impotency.
Pants are bent double
in rigid rows.

I have seen this. It is no hazy, elusive
dream. No, it came to me in a dream
because I heard the soles gasp.

Brass Band

The Salvation Army Band played
on. In expectation. Hands
jammed in pockets, stooped against
the Fifth Avenue chill, I considered
the brass reality: promise
is pain.

Mary knows Christmas and holiday death.
Born in a barn, borne on a cross,
baby boy, God fathered as he was/is
promise fulfilled.

Out there like a star in daylight,
believed, unseen, strolling between
mangers and graves. "Slouching
towards Bethlehem."

The Salvation Army Band played
on, despite the competition.
Anonymity, my lonely companion
walks the crowd like a fish
swimming upstream: full but
not filled.

Good Friday

Shadow flight across stained
windows. Birds on silent
wing, sun shades stealing
light from glass stories.

Trees swaying, leafy limbs
heavy in the wind. Black
moving. God's image. Grave
robbers resurrecting again

the brilliance of the story.
Might the artist have known
when the glass was stained what
would interplay and recreate

another scene?

Paz Says

"Love is a victory over time ..."

Sometimes I can't quite
quiet the primitive, the
part not so free, beneath
radiant rays, where dusk
holds musk. Shadows
mesh like a mist and
cover any hope that this
love will win.

The body thickens slack
changing shape like a
fluid in a sack: Mercury
sad. The only word is
temporal, sight without sound,
no finger tips or nostrils.
Tasteless. So now, my pal
Paz, where is the irrational
power audacious enough
to save my abandonment?

Mackinaw

A single crack will sound for miles. The
bow, black and stained with rust and brine,
will cut the silence, a sharp repeat like
a rifle in a vacant hall.
                    The velvet ice
will yield in violent bursts, broken, heaving,
jutting upward, an awkward bear to fall and
float away; a buoyant piece
                    of a broken whole.
The wind whirls down, spiral bound gust blowing
snow into dervishes dancing beside the ship's
girth. New floe yields swiftly
                    to the bow blade,
but snowberg, thick and deep forces the prow
to buck and slam a mass of tons. Surface and
depth under the violence
                    of the bulky hull
send screaming fissures crying down the frozen
sheet, harbingers of an Advent hymn

If You See The Buddha On The Road, Kill Him.

While at Oxford I ran the river
Isis right, Cherwell, left through
green cloister over gravel graves
of common men. The Saints reposed
in the sanctuary where safe and
scholars hid above the stair,
where nothing banal ever goes.

Churning arms and throbbing veins
salt poured down my soiled
shirt. The fecund scent of meadowed
cows inhaled (with nostrils
flared) the crunch of rock
beneath the waffled soles
I come upon a Buddhist Monk.

He walked alone sandaled in
saffron robe his hands
a knot about his waist, he
flowed beneath the verdant
arch his face a full moon,
bowed toward my passing
blur. A frame too real to

grasp against this August's
sliding night.

Seven Or More

In my cardboard car, the
square tires bumped through
stares too blank for verse.

The quotidian way toward
work, another achromatous day,
sighs too great for words.

Eye corner. Cut quick. Gone now,
but they were balloons. Red.
Seven I count, looking back.

Hearts of Saints tied to
Meters? Someone's breath?
Red balloons. Remember.

See them when you work
your face or pull your
socks. Seven. There were seven,
            or more.

Vine Divine

The last glass of Chard-
onnay is the wisp of that
beautiful color that is
only known as the color of

Chardonnay. A little
bit yellow, a bit copper
colored and described
as white, which means

it includes all colors.
White is the presence
of all colors. Black
is the absence of color.

There could never be a
black wine. Never
say never. Deliver me
from the clarity of ordering

a bottle of black wine.
My last glass of Chardonnay
is golden and from the Vine
of the Divine.

I and Thou

I have been watching the
millennials with the two
handed phone hold and
two thumb rapid type,

not to be an old timer, but
to wonder about the loss
of the "hand written"
and the reduction of con-

versation, with body
language, psychic energy,
eye contact and the spoken
word. Companion derives from

"Com Panis" meaning "With
bread." A companion is one
with whom you break bread.
My fear is that the iPhone

has neither I nor thou ...

Kindergarten Choir

In a small plaster cracked
basement room, I had my
first class in theology. Miss
Bird had us stand to the

Cadence of 1, 2, 3. Miss
Plexico would play the
upright with care. Led
by the manipulation of an

invisible baton, Miss Bird
drew the sacred sound from a chorus
of a kindergarten choir. "Red
and yellow, black and white
They are precious in his sight,
Jesus loves the little child-
ren of the world." Such
an inclusive statement of
the essential Gospel. And

then the final summary
of a theological truth that
still rings true as the
most profound theological
statement that continues
to inform my world-view.
1, 2, 3. Having arisen, we

would incant: "Jesus
loves me, this I know,
for the Bible tells me so."
That is all I know.

Mean End

Eros is the non-rational
desire to connect, re-
late, or create. It is natural,
involuntary, autonomous.

This coin, like most, has
two sides. One leads to
the transcendent, the other
to the sad failure to

scratch desire's itch. Let
us not abandon desire, as
if we could, but to
see it as a means with-

out an end. There are
oscillations between the
means and the end. In
the end, desire means

a path to the Divine. Eros
is not the goal, but the path
that leads where only She
can go: Home/wholeness.

Like all children, each
must find his/her own way.
The poet must get him/her
self out of the way.

Yawn

I don't think work is the
opposite of play. I learned
this when I heard an organist
working the scales, referred
to as, "playing the organ."
Some play at work. The
ball players' work is to
"Play Ball!" Grace is to
find one's work as play. The
opposite of play is not
work, but boredom.
Yawn is the body's
response to lack of
energy for the moment.

My Spring Poem

There must be innumerable
poems about the rebirth of
Spring: Green, blossom, bloom,
tree, leaf, tulip, and flower
wild and tame. So, I will
not compete with plethora
of poems about the opposite
of the Fall. I can't help
reminding me, that the
message is more than nature,
but about my nature. Mother
teaches us once again, that her
wisdom reigns. It rained
last night. It was a hail
storm.

Oxford

I spent an August at
Christ Church College in
Oxford, A.D. 1546.
Tom Tower welcomed
me as I kept a solemn
gait through the gate.
I was Dean of Christ Church

Cathedral, Houston, A.D.
1839. Big deal Dean of
a cathedral, and not
the real deal. Punctured
pretense is the trickster,
that a boy from small
town Oklahoma sits at

high table at an Oxford
College. Especially since
the carpenter taught to
take the lesser place. What
I learned at Oxford was
not academic, or perhaps
it was.

April

Eliott wrote: "April is the
cruelest month." It is the
time when things are dying
to be born. The bulbs planted
in the Fall are struggling to
break the earth's crust.

It is also the time of Easter:
Things are dying to be
born. The dark night of
the soul seeks first
light of new day: Soul
stice.

Forget

Some days I forget. A
man worth his words once
said, "Life is but a
forgetting." Forgetting

is different from repressing.
Forgetting is letting go of
where we come from so when
we return we will "know it

for the first time." Forgetting
is not dementia, but a natural
leaving, for if we remembered
we would hesitantly return.

Children are closer to the Source.
Therefore should be resources
for how to be in the meantime,
the inbetween time, 'til we can

return home. Our hope and
our promise. Don't forget we
have come from some thing to
which we shall return.

Taken For Granted

One gift of age is never
taking for granted a
heart beat or breath drawn.
Isn't it amazing that in

the decades of my life, my
heart has not stopped beating
one time? There will be a time,
but 'til then no, "for granted."

Like a well wound watch
tick after tick, beat and
breath. Mindfulness counts
the box of breath in four

counts in, four counts hold,
four counts exhaled. For counts
held. Granted there is not the
full focus to never take breath and

heartbeat for granted. But when
either lapses, we will be sure
to know which is missing and
not take it for granted.

Cardboard Love

Somehow Valentines Day
seems trivial when contrasted
to the myth of Eros and Psyche.
Cupid was the Roman God.

I prefer Eros, because Hall-
mark cards has made
Cupid a cardboard cherub
chubby and winged.

Eros and Psyche revealed
the rigors of love, of knowing
and being known, courage,
focus and trips to the under-

world. Love is of such
mystery and depth that
we proclaim "God is love." Some
powerful contrast to the card-

board valentines with
hearts and lace, and
chocolates that melt
in the heat.

Ordinary Egg

Butter spray English muffin.
Place on tinfoil-spread
pan. A round of Canadian
bacon circles near.
Enter oven. When
brown, add American
cheese. Break one brown
egg into Teflon pan.
Scramble. Add egg to
muffin and bacon
with cheese. Some like
catsup. This is more
than a meal. It is
a ritual process: extra-
ordinary moment in an ordinary
egg.

So Says The Dream

I heard a dream today where-
in a woman dream figure
instructed a man to go as
far South as he could go

He set out in solitude to follow
his anima's urge. He found
himself at the edge of the sea
Her waves were tongues touching

the rock-lined shore. Cottages
with grey shingles were strong
as they held the wind and
housed the truth of how

all things come of thee, oh
Sea, our maternal womb
and renewing water of re-
birth, so says the dream.

I Now Know

I now know nothing.
Since there may be levels of
knowing, I don't know all
that I know. So, without

knowing all that I know, I
know more than I know.
To be a "know it all," is
not aspired. And yet, in

truth we already know
all that we will ever know.
How do I know that?
There are levels of knowing.
There are levels.
Levels.

I Know What I Like

I don't know plants and trees.
But, like art, I know what
I like ... Peonies. Yes. So
full, abundant, petal on petal.
Georgia O'Keefe art. So, too,
Azaleas. Prefer the pink. I
suppose all plants are feminine.
You know, "Mother Nature."
Crepe Myrtles, Magnolias,
Dog Wood,   Water Oaks, Pecan,
Chinese Elm ... Edna St. Vincent
Millay writes: "Trees are the
only organisms on earth that
seem secure in their place."
I don't know plants and
trees. But I know what
I like. Indian Paint Brush,
Blue Bonnets, Queen Anne's Lace. I
have avoided the Rose, for
she goes without saying. I
don't like Poison Ivy. I know
what I like: Day Lilies.

Q

I saw Q today. I held
him up to amazing
azul eyes. His grin
showed the mirror of de-

light from his grand-
dad. A grandson is he,
mirroring the light from
the Transcendent presence

of love. Of love. Of
love. Grand love.

Spring Break

My son sent me, this day,
a photograph of my high-
school close friend's name, etched
in the black granite of the Viet
Nam Memorial. Nostalgia.
Philip was twenty-one.
A Naval officer. Aircraft
carrier crash. How meaning-
ful. My son knows my
friend through the stories
in my oral history. Thought-
ful. How they would have
loved one another. As one can
see, my namesake sees the
meaning of memory and re-
minds me of love and
loss and the inevitable presence
of both. There is a difference
between sentiment and sentimentality.
Like the difference between a meaningful
moment born from a meaningless death.

My Main Man

Last night I dreamed of an
immense man, statuesque,
noble, regal. My dream ego
walked about this figure.
In the circumambulation,
the me, in the dream, had an
ah-ha! This is the Self!
The true Self, the authentic
Self, the higher Self personified
in this dream-figure. I said
to myself, "Just know he
is here." Such an empowering
image. I'll put that image
in my memory's back pack and
pull it out when I feel small
impotent and lost. This figure
is mental beef jerky, to give
me the energy to continue,
knowing that at the center
and circumference of my
Psyche is this main man.

Saw and See

I grew up land locked. Most
of the bodies of water were man-
made. I had never seen a body
of water where I could not
see the other side. My first

trip to the ocean began on
a bluff in Laguna Beach.
My gaze had no end. I could
not see an opposite shore.
Vast. The Latin is Vastus,

meaning immense. So now
I knew there are things I can-
not see the other side of, so
vast as to void any pretense
of seeing its end or other

side. Oceanic is life
overwhelming and beautiful
like a young man's first
trip to the sea where he
saw what he couldn't see.

Sounds Soothe

Still looking for the little
poem that is not small,
I write: Why do wine,
vine, and Divine rhyme?

Source and Resource

"We don't stop playing because
we grow old; we grow old be-
cause we stop playing."
                    G. B. Shaw

I heard a choir master playing
scales. When, at work, we describe
him as "playing" the organ. Work
and play are not opposites. Many

play at work. One is one's own
authority as to what play might be.
Players know. So, play today,
your way. Never stop, or your

soul will too. Play is what
ever feeds your soul. Sing,
dance, write and draw. Creativity,
is a source for the Creator to

enter creation through the
creature. Play is a re-
source to experience the
Source.

Mosey

I grew up with the word
"mosey." That, in Oklahoma,
was what the cattle did. "Mosey
along little dogie." In a
confusing admonition
little dogies were cattle.
Isn't it interesting that those

who moseyed the cattle
were cowboys? Why weren't
they cowmen? Revelatory.
Cows were dogies, their herdsmen
were boys. Reveals something
about the truth of the South-
western masculine. Cow-

boys, moseying dogies.
The Marlboro Man is
a boy with his dog!
Mosey, a slow movement
toward an uncertain goal.
Like this poem. Maybe
we should learn from
the boy and his dog.

Sole and Soul

It was a windless night.
Yet, the dark held a chill.
Like a tall man with a short
blanket, I could not cover
the contrast of head and
feet. My mentor tells me
the bottom of our feet are
called soles, because that
is where the soul enters the
body, as it could never enter
through the head. So I
cover my soles. Knowing
that the soul is warm,
even if the head is
cold, our essence is covered
like a warm blanket on
a cold night.

Hold And Behold

On a cool crisp day I
wonder what awaits in
the summer steam. Oh,
I know how I must not
allow the future to rob
me of the present. I try.
Mindfulness living is
to live fully in the abundant
moment of the present. But
the past and the future tend
to steal the present. Memory
and imagination, the book-
ends of experience, allow
reverie and fantasy. And
these rob the present. So, I
hold the tension and
learn the difference be-
tween holding and
beholding.

Easter Chill

I sit now at a soccer game
of my grandchild. There is
a chill from an Easter breeze
causing me to hug myself.

He kicks, runs, falls, in
a childhood dance of
life. What is the goal? Not
the square net, or even the
connection of team in
a compete/defeat of
the warrior archetype.
Perhaps the goal is to know

the joy and pain. Such an
Easter chill. Perhaps the
goal is for me to hug
myself, sitting in a
folding chair wondering
what is the goal. Maybe
that is the goal. Or maybe
it is simply a soccer game.

Com Panis
In Memory of Gina Still

Our grandmother's admonition
bore true in you: "No one ever said it would be easy!"
Loss, trauma, accident, illness, injury
were all a part of your too-short journey.

Somehow, your special smile showed us
your soul's depth and a resource from the Source of
all life. You made space and place for hearth and
home. Your nurture was your nature. You fed

us with your bread. Companion derives from the
Latin, "com panis." It means, "with bread." A
companion is one with whom you break bread.
Your bread fed your friendships. Friend *was* your

vocation. A true friend were you, present, knowing,
empathetic, with bouquets of love, all done
under the glow of your soul's smile. We will
always bask in the afterglow of your soul's smile.

Decide

A friend confesses that
she makes her decisions
like the squirrel in the
road. That image helps
us all imagine how we
decide. The Latin "cide"
means to cut or kill. So
to decide, comes from the
same root as homo-
cide and suicide.
No wonder it is difficult
to "decide." Every decision
is death dealing to self
or other. Or it is life
giving to self or
other. How to know?
Authorizing, inner authority,
is to empower one to de-
cide. Each must decide
for each self and have an
inner voice to speak
the decision. Let us not
confuse simple with easy.

Past Time

So, I took a time-out to
ponder the archetypal pattern
of the Hero's Journey in the
American pastime: base-
ball. In Joseph Campbell's
formula of the myth of the
Hero's Journey, he formulates
the three-fold process as symbolic
of the process of individuation.
Baseball is the Hero's Journey.

The Hero emerges from the under-
ground, the dugout. With
lance in hand he stands at
home. In the myth, the three-
fold process is: separation,
initiation, and return.
The Knight takes his lance
and must leave home in order
to return. Someone must
sacrifice to get him home,

lest he die on second. The
ritual is played in a Park.
The park is a derivation
of Paradise. Such is played
out on a diamond, the symbol
of the Self. No wonder we
call it, "America's pastime"
for it is beyond time in the
archetypal pattern of the
Hero's Journey. All seek to
return home, from which we
were called and long to return.

Tiger Hill

In Drumright, Oklahoma,
the only town in which I
ever grew up, there was a
prominent hill, that ran
from the entrance to the
exit through the city's
center. In an instance
of "who knows why?" the
hill was called, Tiger
Hill. God only knows the
number of miles by
foot or pedal I traversed
that prominence.
A parade of memories:
at the hill's foot was
the bank. The owner's
name was Sellers.
Then came Huff's Drug,
where much breath was
huffed about the price
of oil and Friday night
football. So now, here
comes the dime store.
Many a penny I spent
at the 10 cent store.
The grocery store was
the Safe Way. How
reassuring. Next, J. C.
Penny's, where school
clothes were purchased
for more than 10 cents.
Hardware, what
a descriptive name for
the store of hammers,
shovels and drills. Owned
and run by the Smiths.

Such a family history: Black-
smith, Goldsmith— metal
smiths. And next, the
service station. "Filler
up." Mobil, Pegasus, the
flying red horse. We
now have climbed to
the Tower Theater.
Every Saturday I hiked
down to the Tower to
see war movies and
westerns. On the corner
before the Park was the
Drumright Hotel. How
innovative. We stayed
there when I was one. So
the family myth reminds
of our move. Park is a
derivative of paradise.
This space above and below
Center Creek was a poor
derivation. Pedaling up
toward home, pass a few
residences of familiar families.
Then came the Funeral Home.
We used to steal flowers from
their refuse to bury cats
and dogs in a childhood
rehearsal of ritual process.
And now, Felt's Grocery.
This is where my mother
sent me to fetch the for-
gotten and find the
bread and milk, charged
to our account. So
now, the trailer park, where
permanent transients dwelled
in temporary homes forever.

Dr. Neal lived on the
corner of Jones Street,
the street where I lived.
Though he had retired,
and our M.D. was Dr.
Star, a Cherokee medicine
man, Dr. Neal occasionally
checked my throat and
red bumps on my
tender skin. Turn
on Jones Street and at
122 N. is the only
house in which I
ever grew up. Take
a trip up Tiger Hill,
and you will know:
that which is most
personal is most universal.
This poetic piece in-
vites you to travel
from Main Street. Any
more instruction would
be pedestrian.

Radish

Still looking for the
little poem that is
not small, I write:
See the thin sliced radish,
red and white, salted
on buttered bread.

What Is In A Name?

What is in a name? My
mother was the seventh of
seven children. Each of
whom was delivered by
Dr. James Pittman. Her
sixth sibling was named
after the deliverer of all
her children. I was named
after him, my mother's
beloved brother. I am
also James Pittman. A
few years ago, I made
pilgrimage to my mother's
birthplace. Turning into
the town square, I turned
onto James Pittman
Drive. All in a moment, I
knew I came from a story.

In Ireland, the person who
goes in to the under mine is
called a "pitman." I am
a priest and analyst. I go
into the under-mind. Go
figure. What is in a
name?

Where Have All The Children Gone?

Where have all the children gone?
Growing up before T.V., computer
and iPhone, my brother
and I lived outside. Yard
games, staged plays, exploration,
grass, trees, wildflowers, nature's
natural tapestry— a backdrop
of life lived out, outside.

There, we human animals
connected with other animals:
dogs, cats, cows, horses, chickens,
snakes, turtles and frogs.
And of course, we encountered
the insects, ants, and centipedes,
for better or worse. We led cows
and rode horses. Butch Gibson's mother

taught us to milk cows. Run,
jump, leap, skip didn't
seem like exercise. Our
punishment for ill deeds
done was to have to stay
in the house all day. And
now, children have the
oxymoron of "planned
play." With maids, butlers
and chauffeurs as parents,
these independent dependents

move from house to school,
by car, and then to an
activity without imagination.
So, now, I am tired of my
own voice of comparison.
Tradeoffs there are with

the gift of the internet
and convenience technology
has endowed us. I think

now, I will close and
dissert the opine whine and
go outside and play.

Distant Wheat

Still looking for the
little poem that is
not small, I write:
My grandson's hair
is the color of distant
wheat.

Love And Hate

It is all about energy. There
is no difference between
the energy in the Universe
and psychic energy. Each
psyche is a quantum of
energy. Our life experience
is in how the energy gets
constellated, experienced and
articulated. Sometimes the
energy is called "love." Some-
times the energy is called "hate."
Same energy, just a different
time and temperature. At
times we experience both
at the same time. Maybe
love and hate are not opposites,
just strong energy from a
deep attachment. Hard to
hate someone you don't love.

Doxology

A doxology is a short hymn
of praise. Perhaps we might
try doxological living. Making
our entire being express an
attitude of gratitude. "Praise
God from whom all blessings
flow," is a doxology. I
like the word "flow." Pour
down, like a stream, or rain or
tears. Tears tell us a little and
a lot. Sorrow and joy bring
a flow of tears. Each tear
is a drop of doxology. Even
in sorrow we can be grate-
ful for that which we mourn.
There is a baptism in
tears, cleansing and healing.
Blessings flow. We can
laugh 'til we cry. I suspect
the opposite is true, too. Some
where in this poem is a short
hymn of praise.

Music To Save Our Soul

"Bye, bye, Miss American
pie" ... so the plaintive call
of 1971, in a prophetic voice
lamented, "the day the music died."
"Do you believe in rock and roll?
Can music save your soul?"

We in the "Chevy at the levee,"
we learned that popular
culture reflects our
collective anxiety about
change, loss, uncertainty.
This ballad validates a time

when we looked to
music to save our
soul. Maybe the 1971
plea is always the eternal
now ... the loss of which is:
"This will be the day
that I (we) die."

Sacred In The Profane

I flew to Ireland today. Tomorrow
I will traverse the Emerald Isle
from Dublin to Galway. I have
never been here, in this life.

My roots are in this soiled
soil. I am a romantic. When
I imagine this place I see a
green sea, undulating, rolling
hills with grassy knolls and
a historic Book of Kells.

Celtic spirituality is bred
in my bones. They taught a
natural spirituality whereby
nature held, if not concealed,
the transcendent. They also pre-
dated the quantum physicists.
The quantums assert that there are not

three dimensions, but maybe as
many as eight or nine.
They further opine that on
occasion one dimension
"bleeds" into the other. The
Celts knew that at certain
places, the "curtain between
the realms is very thin."

I am now in Ireland.
My romantic self is in
ecstatic anticipation. The
fact is, I write this in a
Radisson Inn that looks
like every Airport Inn
in the soiled soil of all

unholy ground in the
profane world. Help me
find the sacred in the pro-
fane!

Alliteration Aside

This Irish pub has a
sense of place. It
presents without pretense,
that those who sit at bar

are welcome. A row
of pulls fetch the
pub's brew. A keep
wears white shirt with

black vest and sleeve
garters. No small talk,
as his towel dries the
glasses that hold the whiskey.

He intuits, from my
accent, that I am a guest.
He offers concern in the form of
a question. "First time to

the island?" My nod
is met with a smile,
as he twists the towel
removing, minute moisture.

"You'll be findin' your
way." A packed proposition
to ponder. Alliteration
aside, there is a truth

in the tender wisdom
of the man who keeps
the bar and pours forth
the Spirits.

Galway Bay

I cannot resist: Today is a
gray day on Galway Bay.
Irish mist holds mystery
on an Isle with a tradition

of natural spirituality.
Celts held nature as the
mother of mystery. She
is birthing such in this

gray.   Truth is not black
or white, but layered in
delicate shades of gray.
The white caps on the

dark sea merge quickly
on the gray bay. There
are places where the
curtain between the

realms is very thin.
So it is in the midst of
the mist— heaven on
Earth.

In Ireland

In Ireland, I am struck
by the plethora of stone
fences and green hedges.
Territorial they, and with
an abundance of stones they
throw them in intricate
stacks making mandalas across
the verdant land. Now add
fluffy white flocks of sheep
to the squared land of green,
and one is in Ireland. If
hills can roll they are rolling
here. In a stretch of time
one cannot escape the land-
scape of stone fence, green
hedge, white fleece, and
all of this, followed any
way, will lead to the deep
blue sea. Landscape leads
to seascape, inescapable
in Ireland.

Stone And Scone

Stones and scones are the
Irish fare. On Aran Island
there are millions of polished,
rounded stones. Stones honed by

eons of water and wind.
Much of Irish identity is
found in the solid soul of
longevity in the stones.

Scones are the frequent fare
of the biscuit at tea. Flakey,
shall we say, with fruit, raisin
or cherry, this layered taste is

designed to assist the tea
into the ritual process of the
honed, scone incarnating
the taste of Heaven in a simple

fare. Fair enough? Let us
beware of when the Irish
confuse the two and the
scone is a stone, a hard
truth to swallow!

Onomatopoeia

Just returned from Ireland,
such a land of onomatopoeia:

babbling brooks, bleating sheep,
and an occasional caw of a

black crow, the pluck of a
harp string. One thinks of

the island sights, but
at the coast, the roar of

the wave, the shrill sound
of the swirling wind, the

chug of the island ferries,
Ireland in its fullness, is

onomatopoetic. No wonder
there are so many Irish poets.

Good Shepherd ★

Father Abbot Timothy Sweeny
of St. Meinrad Monastery
tells a story of substance.
He made a pilgrimage to
Jerusalem. While there, on
a free afternoon he de-
cided to hire a driver to
take him to see a shepherd
working his flock. He was,
in the priestly vocation,
a symbolic shepherd.

As luck would have it,
his driver took him to
a small hill overlooking
a pasture full of sheep and
a singular shepherd. Even
more luck ensued. A lamb
strayed from the flock, like
the parable. The shepherd left
the ninety and nine to seek
the one lost. When the good
shepherd found the stray he

picked the lamb up by
his ears and kicked him
in the ass, sending him
sternly back to the flock.
"That," Father Sweeny said,
"is the true nature of the
Good Shepherd."

At The Well

The amount of water one
gets depends on the size
of the bucket one brings.

We are a thimble people.
With oceans of water at
our living wells, we
will die of thirst, before

building more abundant
buckets. Our expectation
are low, our consciousness
limited. And life's juice

is a dry river bed longing
for living waters of experience.
We build bungalows on
foundations that are designed

for tremendous towers. So
no judgment. Labor and
pain accompany birth,
so too, blood. So we

miss the fullness re-
main unfulfilled and
build no bigger buckets
and miss the wellspring.

George

My granddog is George.
Rescued. Neurotic in a
kind of appealing way.
He is a snowball, with

an intense desire to
make tactile, bodily,
eye contact. He will
snoop his nose under

my hand for a stroke.
Abandoned, he, of course,
has an abandonment complex.
Anxious alone, but so ex-

cited to belong. By now
the strokes of love have
quieted his anxiety of aband-
onment. When he is present

I feel valued, known and
wanted. All the things he
so longs to have from
me. George. George!

Four X Grand

Still looking for the
little poem that is
not small, I write:
grand means impressive,
in size or effort: I have
four Grand children.

Liquid Dark

I have heard the dark referred
to as a liquid, that pours down

the horizon at dusk. In Northport,
at sunset, we hurry in golf carts

to the dock to see the pour.
The delicate shades of pink and

blue provide the colorful
preface to the liquid dark. It

happens every night. Every night
it happens for the first time. The

sun sets slowly
'til he puts his head on the

horizon's pillow. Then dark
descends like a liquid and

starts a solar snooze. Shortly,
the lunar sister reflects his absence.

Orchid Core

What is that delicate butterfly-
like little center to an orchid?
Sometimes, instead of wings, it
looks like a harp, maybe to
be played by a butterfly. Wings
and strings rest nestled into the
core of an orchid. Of course, the
whole plant is an angel,
with heavenly wings. Orchids
are ordinary and extraordinary.

Allie

My second granddog
is Allie. She leaps.
Enter her home, she
runs to your side in an

enthusiastic, eager,
ebullient embrace.
She could be the dog
by the megaphone

listening to "her mentor's
voice." She is a 1930s
canine. White with
black mask, Charlie

Chaplin's dog. She
loves to tussle with
her human brothers
who are more animal

than she. After the
leap, embrace and tussle,
I rest on the sofa and
she brings a soft embrace.

She curls, as in a nest,
and rests her head on
my thigh. Blinks her
eyes in a subtle se-

duction and I hum,
"Good girl. Such a good
girl." She tilts her head
and flirts for more.

Flowering

Still looking for the
little poem that is
not small, I write:
A rose, arose.

Breeze

How many breezes are there?
Summer breeze, cool, gentle,
calm. Breeze is a meta-
phor for love. Must be, be-
cause that gentle blow is
a natural paradox of that
which cools the body, warms
the heart. I love sitting
at my grandson's baseball
game with the comfort of
a spring breeze at our
backs as the boys breeze
around the bases. This
slight wind is a fresh
air that refreshes.

Crabbing

Today at noon, I ate a crab
cake. Light breading, stout
remoulade, lumpy. A mean-
ingful memory flew through.

When my sons were boys
we took the ferry to Bolivar
Peninsula. There we
crabbed. A chicken neck

on a stout string, thrown
past the rocks: crab bait.
Claws clung to the chicken
hook. A large burlap

bag held the catch. Dad's
pliers kept claws off of
little fingers. The fun
turned to chore as we

picked the meat from the
shell. Then delight, when
at dusk we ate crab cakes.
Light breading, stout remoulade,
lumpy.

Tame Flower

Blake writes of a certain
consciousness that can,
"see heaven in a wild
flower." I know he
would agree that heaven
is in our tame flowers, too.

Peonies. Heaven. Pink,
purple petals. They are
so feminine: Mother Nature's
breasts. Hydrangeas. There

is a photo of me in front of
my grandmother's house in a
galvanized tub. I, nude
at six months, the white

tub held a red ring.
The picture's backdrop
is a hydrangea bush.
Though the photo is in

black and white, I re-
member them as blue. I
was in heaven.

Ringing True

At eight, I saw my mother
wring a chicken's neck.
Such a sight to see. I
know the saying, "running
around like a chicken with
its head cut off." A white
ball with yellow feet and
a red ring where its neck
and head had rested. The body,
still with instinct, circles
and flaps, panic and pain,
without a brain. Impossible?
Not what I saw, when at
eight, my mother took a
feathered fowl and held it
above her head and like
a lasso, she circled
her arm, till the bird's
neck under torque, gave
way to gravity. This was
no violent act of death.
It was a maternal ritual
of nurture. In nature
organisms must die
for humans to live.
This wringing was
the initiation of a platter
of my mother's fried chicken.

Image and Imagination

Most of the things I think I
know, I imagine. I know
nothing of wine. But, I
imagine that grape, ripe
and ready, plucked from

the vine, pressed into
service and aged to my glass.
But the process isn't the point.
That pearl of a fruit holds
within a taste and spirit

to alter consciousness even
at an altar. Imagine
the small spherical fruit can
hold the essence of life. It
sacrifices itself in order to

symbolize the ultimate
sacrifice. This is my deep
knowledge, I imagine.

Sweater

Though this is not "May Day,"
it is a day in May. Stepping
on my deck, I felt a late
Spring chill. Today's temp
will be in the low 60's.
This morning at the closet
I chose a sweater, because
I could and because this
day in May may be the
last sweater day 'til
late Fall. What is it about
sweaters? Warmth, embrace,
security, must be maternal.
My mother/sweater held well.
Tonight, I peeled her off
and folded her gently into
the night, knowing if I
need her again she will
unfold into my arms.
I rest assured.

Synesthesia

Who knows why I see
numbers as having colors.
One is white, four blue, five
red, nine black, ten white.
I never concerned myself with
this, 'til I read an article on
synesthesia. We synesthetes
see numbers, as colors. Evidently
not all people do. How
could five not be red? Don't
you love the human brain/mind?
I am told that a childhood trauma
can cause (must I write again?)
synesthesia. One gift of
my near death experience as
a child is that four is
blue and five is red.

Breadth of Breath

The Hebrews called it "ruach."
It means wind or spirit. One
can hear it as the "breath of
God," or Divine Inspiration.
In Latin, inspire derives from
in (into) plus spirare (breathe). To
be inspired is to have the
breath of the Divine blowing
through you.

I remember when I smoked,
enjoying the sight of my
breath. And now, on cold
mornings, when I go to get
the newspaper, to be surprised
by the sight of my breath.
Some say that the peace pipe,
and circled rituals of
peyote, are rehearsals of
inspiration seen in the ex-
haled smoke. At the very
least we can see, that the
invisible exists, even when
unseen. And how inspiring
when we can see the un-
seen. This is the breadth
of breath.

Spice Of Life

A colleague, at breakfast
asked to, "pass the pepper."
She needed the spice to speckle
her grits. "I don't want to

live in a world without pepper."
In truth, as long as she was alive
the world would not be without
spice. How for granted we take
the spice of life. Tell me what
enhances your taste for living?
Tell me of that bit of stimulation

that sets your tongue to lick
life. Keep at hand, in your
back pack granular and
glandular speckle that give

your grits gravitas. Make it
a ritual process of calling on
your pepper shaker to enhance
the tasteless, banal, and insipid.
Shake it up! Pour the pepper.
Now, enjoy the ground zest in a
new season.

Stir

Still looking for the
little poem that is
not small, I write:
I can hear the butterfly
stirring in a cocoon.

Bush And Thorn

I awaited the rain drops. The
grass prayed for rain. The
sound of such on my tin
roof takes me somewhere
special. Rain reigns. So
like all idealized, romanticized
reflections, too much of any-
thing is violence. A
violent rain fell spelling
flood. The whelm was
over. And then the water
rise stopped where it rose.
Rise. Rose. Some thought.
No rose is without thorns,
yet God gave us memory
so we could have roses in
the winter. Rise, rose.
The rising water brought
the summer roses. No wonder
the sound of the drops on my
roof were harbingers of beauty,
bush and thorn.

Bard Of The Front Yard

We had very little back
yard, at least in fact. So life
was played out in the
front yard. The sidewalk
worked, though cracked. The
street was dust. Trees formed
a trellis, an archway for few
who traversed down Jones
Street. It was not a street
to nowhere, but the where
people went was the rodeo
grounds, or Whitlock Park.
Park in name only. Scruffy
shrubs, little grass,
swing sets with rusted
chains and split seats.

So the conscious world
lived in the natural earth
at night we would spread quilts
on her breast and lie back
in her embrace and stare
at stars. We would wonder,
sometimes aloud, about the
wonder. Wonderful! Mosquitoes
and chiggers would bite
us out of awe, into the
realization that Mother Nature
can heal or steal. One of
her natural sides does not
eliminate the other. Actually
she acts fully in the presence
of her presents of both the
insight and the bite. All
of this wisdom came from
a quilted repose in the
front yard. And from the
bard of the front yard.

A Bridge Across

Sitting at the bar an obvious
observation occurs. The bar
is an altar. I will order the
bruschetta and chardonnay.
The liturgical stone table
is the place of feeding and
transformation. With an
appropriate invocation, there
appears a presence that is
present everywhere for those
who have the eyes to
see. The body and blood
can be remembered and
that which is remembered
is present. Re-member that
which is dismembered.
Similar is not same, but
truth is a bridge across.

Peel/Appeal

She struggles with the orange.
There is a cardboard crate
of them. Each unique, each
the same: round, asymmetrical,
and of course, orange.

She tends bar. Bent forward
she selects the best. Even-
tually they will be a peel.
A curl of rind taken from
a fruit that was born to

dress a drink, and to share
a sensuous sense of color,
texture and taste. Thank
you for tending the table
where our senses open us

to a fruit that appeals.

Color of Copper

I saw the copper color of my
drink. Truth be known the
drink is to alter consciousness.
Altered from the uncertain
anxiety of being human. But
tonight, for a reason, I see the
copper color. Maybe it is
to show that there are natural
ways to assuage anxiety: colors—
who would have thought
that which soothed the agita-
tion was the color copper.
It was the color copper.

Wonder Bread

So, I am told, in order to
lose weight, we must
forego bread. What? In
our rational brain we

analyze the caloric,
protein rich, protein
poor and conclude the
body's response to bread.

This staff of life holds
more meaning than the
waistline. What a waste.
Sensuous, symbolic,

tantalizing to the tongue.
In certain circles it is
sacramental. Born and
bred to eat bread. Why

can't life be so simple, as
to know that bread is the
stuff of life, as long as we
don't stuff ourselves.

Silken Threads

My grandmother had a
vegetable garden whereby
we learned that a tomato
is a fruit. She would
put on a pot of boiling water,
sprinkle salt, and send us to
the garden to pull ears of
sweet corn. With the hands
of an artist, she would
strip the corn, pulling the
silken threads
in a musician's grace and,
"plop," the ear entered its
transformation.

A fresh ear of corn. Teeth,
crunch, juice, swallow the
yellow kernels and know
that the Grand Mother was
not just my mother's mother,
but Mother Nature. She
came to me in my grand-
mother, in a garden, with
sweet corn, in a two-hand
held cobb! And a sensuous
sound of my teeth securing
the kernels into my interior
space, knowing that sweet
corn is a symbol and fact.

Maternal Metaphor

I long for a day like today.
90% chance of rain, the
sky is a canopy of del-
icate shades of gray. It

is as though Mother is
pregnant and about to birth.
When the waters break
and cleanse, new life

breathes a fresh breath.
The thunder sounds the
energy of the lighting's
enlightenment. Lest I

get possessed by the ro-
mantic moment, birth
causes pain and labor,
so somewhere near, the

lightning strikes, wind
blows a bold breath
and turns the temporary
over, only to grow again.

Nature is first a fact,
and only then she is a
metaphor ... a maternal
metaphor.

Bad Dad

Such a sight to see my
four grands dancing, laughing
and playing right in front
of me. Not conscious of
the animation they bring to
this Granddad. When Finn
could barely talk, I tried to
get him to say, "Granddad."
He echoed, "Bad Dad." The
first born gets naming rights.
I am "Bad Dad." I am good
bad, not evil. Somehow poetic
justice rules. Such a sight
to see, four grands, animating
a Bad Dad, what a sight to
see. Beauty and Bad Dad,
a good deed, indeed.

A Moth On A Cloth

Through the curtain's
gauzy cloth, I saw
the shadow of a moth.
Day's first light framed

a winged silhouette.
Is it a shadow, or
an unveiled dark spirit
revealing the eternal

presence of light and dark?
They are after all nature's
twins to conspire to
inspire with a moth

framed on a curtain's
cloth. As different as
night and day and
as alike as they

can play to frame a
moth on a cloth

The Way

The scene is fully set.
Familiar setting, like
one's own living room.
I rise to lecture.

Don't like the word or
concept of lecture. Synonyms:
share, talk, speculate, wonder,
confess, reveal, seek, conceive,

bleed? They have come to
hear, but that single sense
is not enough. Blake says:

"The senses are the inlets of
the Soul." They must see, taste,
touch, smell and source the
sixth sense to find and feel

whatever it is for which I am
a conduit. The best way is to
get myself out of the way.
That is the way.

Street Sounds

So the sounds are all
poetic. Street sounds
make poems. The sibilance
of the bus tire turning on
the moist pavement. The
jack hammer pounds a
poem in rhythm. All rhyme.
The bounce of a basketball in
the driveway court. The
sound of the siren in its
shrill, painful tone.
And most poignant is the
sound of the train whistle
sad, lonely and yet warm
and soothing especially
at night in bed. Extra-
ordinary sounds in the
ordinary.

Divine Tickle

I write many poems about
the extraordinary in the ordinary.
Redundant? Is the regular
Spring bloom redundant, be-
cause it repeats itself?

Is the goodbye kiss every
day repetition, or a re-
hearsal of touch? When
the Eagles sing, "Hotel
California," are they re-

peating themselves? Or
are they singing their song?
When my granddaughter giggles,
is she making a similar sound
again, or is she sounding

the sound of a Divine tickle?
I end now for fear of repeating
myself. Or am I re-minding
of the importance of paying attention
to the extraordinary ...

Finite/Infinite

Two letters can change
a world view. Take finite
and infinite. One cries
"no" the other screams,
"yes." Everything leads to
an end and two letters
later it begins again.
Can two things be true
at once? "All good things must
come to an end." The end
is, "world without end."

So, which word informs
your view? It is infinitely
more open to rest assured
in the infinite than to
be assured of a rest at the
finite. There are only two
letters difference, therefore
one is contained in the other.
Both may be true. Here I
end and begin.

Dry Whole

It is said, "when one ceases
to drink from a well, it
dries up." It is said that when
a Grandfather sees his grandchild

for the first time, his eyes
"well up." Wet must be
healthy or shall we say
"well." Water cleanses,

heals, sustains, renews,
and satiates. A symbol
and fact that we must
drink from the well of

life lest we die from
a dry whole.

Morning And Mourning

When did you first learn
that a "morning dove" was
a "mourning dove?" I
had heard their plaintive calls

as part of life's lament,
first right out my open
window as a child. Perched
on limbs and power lines,

their wings made a whistling
sound as they flew down
to forage for seeds. I asso-
ciate them with the smell

of gardenias. Four feet tall,
the bush was level with
my window sill. Fragrance.
Doves descending, redolent

sense of the presence. A child
awakens to the presence of
a descending dove, and a sweet
smell of life. And now

mourns the loss of innocence
when the favorite sport of
some adults is to dove hunt.
Mourning the morning dove.

Deeper

Since a child, I have
always tried to find some-
thing to look forward
to. Now in my fourth

quarter, I have learned
to look forward to the
next moment. Maybe
even, not move forward.

The Dalai Lama was
asked what was his favorite
moment in his life?
He responded, "This one."

Being in the moment sends
me neither backward
nor forward, but deeper.

Naturally

We use Nature to describe
our nature. "It dawned
on me ..." "It was a
nightmare ... " We all

know of mountain top
experience, dessert time,
plateaus. And what of
body metaphors? "Get off

my back," "pain in the neck,"
"you broke my heart ..."
Nature is our nature
most of what we experience

is natural. Even that which
isn't natural is contrasted
to natural: "supernatural" or
"unnatural." So shall

we say everything we ex-
perience is natural?

Progress/Regress

We do not graduate from
a developmental stage.
We accumulate them.
I am still two and

fourteen. I can re-
gress to those ages in
an eye's blink. Some-
times for good and others

for ill. Sometimes
consciously and most
times not. Verse and
reverse, progress re-

gress, if we take two
steps forward and
one back we are moving
forward ... or we are

dancing.

Wonder Child

When I was a child
I was distracted by
wonder. Wonderful!
To be distracted by
wonder is to lay judge-
ment aside, to simply
let it live its natural
way, and to wonder.
Nature is the mother of
wonder: sunshine, gray
day, cool breeze, hail
storm, snow, rain,
fire. To warm and burn
no judgement, no jury
to convict, just the
distraction of wondering.
Mother Nature is the
maternal nurture of
the wonder child.

Toast

The scribe tries to di-
scribe a scene. Don't
you love words? Dis-
scribe sounds like to
erase a picture. Now
we are trying to draw
a picture with words:
a slice of bread toasted
brown, moist with the
melted butter, brittle
at the crust and sponge
soft at core. The contrast
tickles the tongue. It
is called taste. Pressed
between the mouth's roof
and the tongue's buds
there is a sensual sound
of a smack. This is
the description of a
toast.

Stand Under

How shall we not
hide the things that
open us to pain? One
who seeks pain is path-
ological. We who seek
to avoid pain are
natural nomads, wandering
and wondering why all
must suffer. "Suf" means
from below; "fer" comes
from "ferre": to carry.
To suffer is to carry from
below— to stand under,
'til we can, "understand."
Pain and suffering are
opportunities for new
understandings. I am
not happy that that is
true. Understand?

Conclusion

Can we not conclude?
Does that mean end? Or
does that mean surmise?
Can we conclude? What
is your conclusion? Shall
we collude to conclude?
This word play, though
playful, runs its course
quickly. Can we not
conclude that this line
will be our conclusion?
Such a nice surmise!

Long To Belong

Particles. They sound apart,
but are, after all, a part
of the whole. Do they
know? Does each know
they are not apart, but
a part? No. Not all know.
Those who do, do their
part. Those who don't
are set apart to trouble
the whole, in their longing
to belong. So, let us now
renew our call to include,
so that the fragments
might seek one another
in order to make a
whole.

Words On A Page

Updike wrote that he
began to write because,
he liked the way the
words looked on the page.
Shapes appeal to the
eye. There must be some-
thing about symmetry that

assuages the anxiety that
arises with chaos, fragmen-
tation and the daily vicissitudes.
Constellating wholeness
the mandala, a squared
circle, soothes the ego's
anxious fear of the unknown.

So, pay attention to the
attendant symmetry that
can be seen with a
simple word, swirled
and turned on an ordinary
page with companion words
penned on a page as a poem.

Resound

When I hear words that
resonate with that
deep full reverberating
sound of similarity,

I must look up and
wonder: Like, presence
and presents. Clearly,
presence of love, presence

of the transcendent, presence
of mystery and meaning are
presents. They must be re-
ceived and unwrapped.

Presence is a present. So
what then is absence?
Sorry, I could not abstain
from abstinence. Lest we

think they are opposites,
absence can be a present.
This is similarity without
sound.

Orchids

Still looking for the
little poem that is
not small, I write:
Orchids are not plants,
they are planets.

Close

Time to close, which
means to end. Close also
means to be near. We
are close to a close.

The end is near. When
I say close, I mean to
gather, hug, hold, connect.
Close, as near the end,

must be kept in a closet.
We hold together, because
we know the end is always
near. Come over here, come

in close, you never know
when the near might end.
Live in the present, come
close, hold on, and let go.

Underpass

I was to speak in Houston
Thursday night. Mid-night
the thunder storm echoed the
forecast: torrential rains all
day tomorrow. What to do?
Driving three hours in a
torrent sets anxiety at
a fast pace. The airports:
delayed. My sense of re-
sponsibility in competition
with my sensibility created
a clear conflict. I, in a
healthy/neurotic decision
chose to go. Blinded by
rain, the trailer trucks,
when in front, were
car washes. Seeking the
yellow line, not down
my back, but by being
on the highway oriented
the anxious ego. My great
fear was the flood on
Westpark underpass. I ob-
sessed much of the way
about whether, because of
the weather, the under-
pass would be free. I
took the turn, traveled
the tollway and when
I arrived at the feared
flood of the underway,
it was dry, free, open,
available. In that moment
I knew that all my anxiety
about being blocked was
wiped away like the

rhythm of the wind-
shield wipers: heart
beat, and breath, casting
away anxiety: the fear
of the unknown. I spoke
Thursday evening, bold
steadfast and unafraid.

Porch View

As I sit on my screened porch in Northport Point,
I see, on Grand Traverse Bay, the Hornpipe with
Her red hull and in a harbor furl. She is tethered
Tightly to a Great Lake. Behind her is a stone
Bridge, leading to a stoney point. The water
Colors run from aquamarine to forest green.
On the Stoney point, on summer nights, young
People build fires, drink beer and sing, "I feel the
Winds of God today."

CPSIA information can be obtained
at www.ICGtesting.com
Printed in the USA
LVOW08s1608030417
529439LV00005B/1290/P